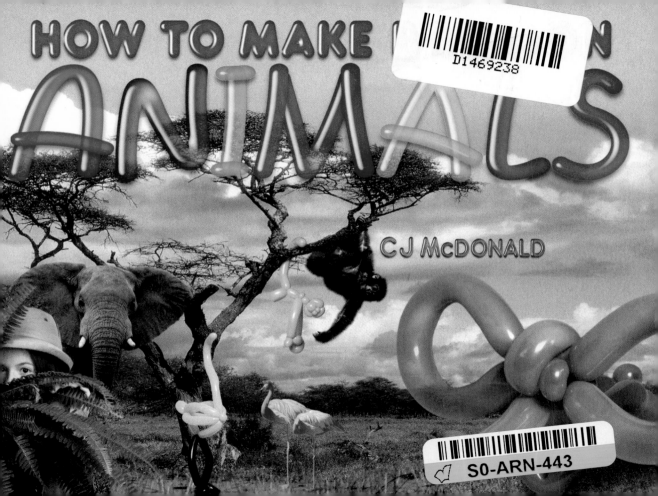

HOW TO MAKE BALLOON
ANIMALS

CJ McDonald

S0-ARN-443

With thanks for the contributions of P.J. the clown, who puts fun in the air, and to my husband and children, who haven't burst my bubble.

Author: CJ McDonald
Designed by Bill Henderson

an imprint of
■SCHOLASTIC
www.scholastic.com

Scholastic and Tangerine Press and associated logos are trademarks of Scholastic Inc
Published by Tangerine Press, an imprint of Scholastic Inc;
557 Broadway; New York, NY 10012

10 9 8 7 6 5 4 3 2 1

ISBN 0-439-68024-7
Printed and bound in China

MAKE AN AIR PET!

Bring out the party animal in your friends by creating your own inflatable zoo! Before long, you'll be able to tame a shark, grab a gator by the tail, make a turtle fast, get a leg up on an octopus, or make a monkey for your uncle. You'll be the top dog!

These are animals with a twist, so first take time to learn the basics. With a little practice, you'll soon become master of your own menagerie.

C'mon, let's unleash your animal instincts!

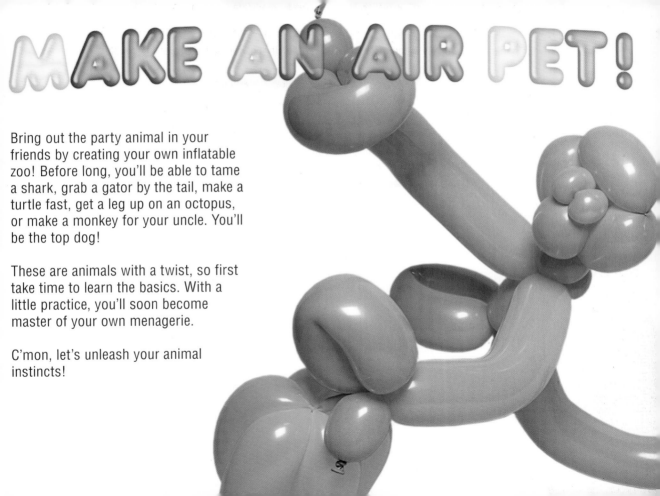

CONTENTS

Difficulty Scale

Easy   Medium   Tricky

Pump Primer

Your kit contains everything you need to start your own miniature zoo! Your pets begin with a pump and long, skinny balloons called 260s. If you run out of balloons, don't sweat it. Just make a trip to your nearest party store.

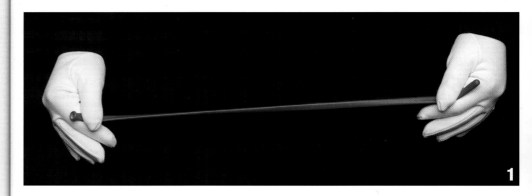

1) Before you pump your balloons, take a stretch. Grab a balloon by either end. The closed end is the "tail," and the open end is the "nozzle." Now, stretch the balloon across your chest. This gives it extra length and makes it, well, stretchier – both of which make it easier to work with.

2) Next, gently slide the nozzle end – the open end, remember? – over the tip of the pump. Holding the balloon onto the tip with your opposite hand, start pumping with the other hand. Keep pumping until you have a tiny stub (1/2 inch, or 1.25 cm) at the other end. That stub is a pop-preventer. If you blow up a balloon all the way, it just may blow up! So, for safety reasons, never fully inflate a balloon.

Holding the nozzle with one hand, carefully slide it off the pump with the other, pinching it together about 2 inches from the nozzle as it is released.

3) Let the air out to the point of the pinch, holding it tightly between your fingers. You've just burped your balloon! Now tie off the nozzle, and you're ready to take a turn at twisting!

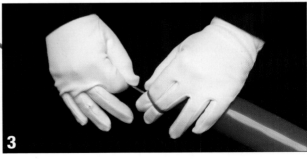

7

Take a Turn at Twisting

To be king over your animal domain, remember that practice rules. Start by pumping up a few 260s, some with tails and some with stubs. Now it's time to practice twisting.

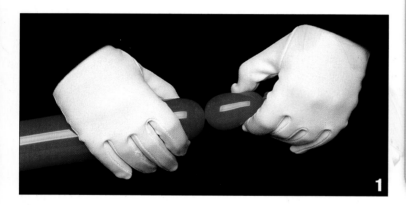

Most of the balloons in this book call for tails – and not just because animals have 'em. "Tail" refers to uninflated end of a balloon – sometimes a stub, sometimes several inches, depending on how many twists go into the pattern. Just leave uninflated whatever length tail is required, and tie off.

Bubble

1) This one is easy. To make a 1-inch (2.5-cm) bubble, hold your balloon by the knotted end. Using your other hand, pinch your fingers down about an inch from the nozzle. Then twist. You have a bubble. Always hold the first and last bubbles in a series; and remember that you must always twist in the same direction, or you'll undo your previous twists.

Loop twist

1) Here's a technique you'll use often to make ears or legs. Hold your 1-inch (2.5-cm) bubble with one hand, and make a 4-inch (10-cm) bubble just beyond it. Remember always to hold your first and last bubbles – in this case, your first and second.

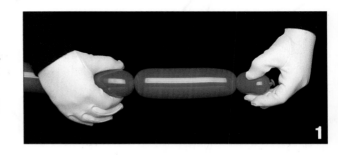

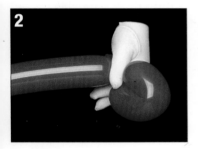

2) Fold the 4-inch (10-cm) bubble in half so the beginning twist and the last twist line up.

3) Twist the ends together at the joints to form a 2-inch (5-cm) loop twist. In our patterns, the size of the loop twist is the length of each side.

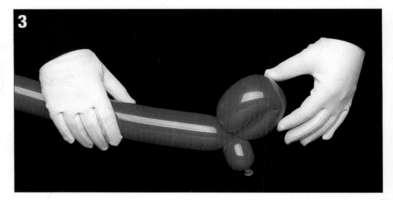

Some patterns call for specific dark colors, such as black. Trouble is, when balloons are uninflated, it's hard to tell the difference between black, purple, green, or blue. So here's a handy tip: Pump a tiny bit of air into the very tip of a balloon to determine its color before starting your project.

Lock twist

1) Make a 2-inch (5-cm) bubble and two 3-inch (7.5-cm) bubbles just beyond the loop twist. Fold the 3-inch bubbles down.

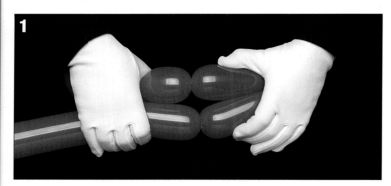

2) Twist the bubbles together at the joints. Say "stay," and it will obey!

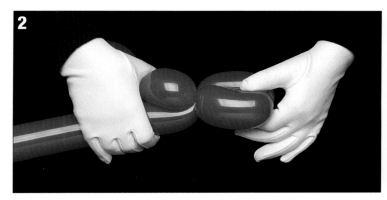

Tulip twist

1) Using another 260, hold the balloon with one hand. Using the other, push the nozzle into the balloon using the forefinger of your other hand. Pinch down on the nozzle with your other hand, pulling your index finger out of the nozzle.

2) Then make a 1-inch (2.5-cm) bubble. Poof! Your nozzle has disappeared!

Curl

1) Here's a handy trick for shaping necks, horns, or trunks. Using the same or another 260, coil the balloon like a hose, starting at the nozzle end. Squish it down a little to increase its turning curve.

2) Now release it. What a way to shape up!

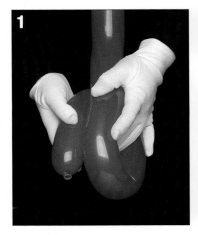

Soften

1) Many patterns require you soften the balloon. This gives the balloon more "give" when you're doing lots of twists and decreases the "pop factor." Using a balloon with at least a 1-inch (2.5-cm) tail, gently squeeze the air from the middle of the balloon . . .

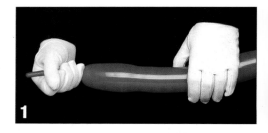

2) . . . to the end.

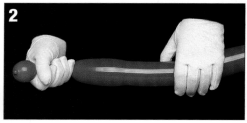

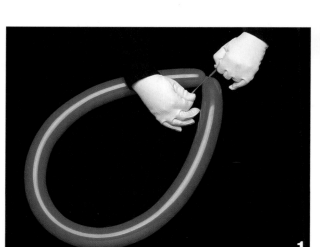

Circle twist

1) Using the 260 you just softened, hold the tail in one hand and the nozzle in the other. Tie them together in a knot. You have the perfect shape for the base of wings or ears for larger air pets.

Twist

1) Holding the circle twist in one hand, pinch your thumb and forefinger together at the center of the balloon.

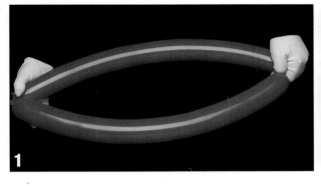

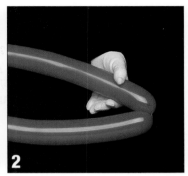

2) Twist at that point.

Ear twist

1) This trick locks a bubble in place and also gives your creations a neater finish, but it does take some practice. Make a 1-inch (2.5-cm) bubble in the middle of your circle twist.

2) Then pinch it – go ahead – between your thumb and forefinger. Pull it up, and twist it around.

PRETTY IN PINK

Put on some shades and you'll soon have it made, but don't keep it wading long!

1) Inflate two pink 260s with 1/2-inch (1.25-cm) tails and one black 260 with a 1/4-inch (.6-cm) tail.

2) Using one of the pink 260s, do a circle twist (p.11), creating a loop.

3) Find the center of the loop, and twist (p.11).

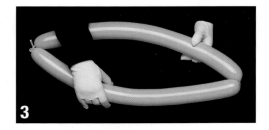

4) Find the center again, and twist off.

5) Make a football shape by folding the loops inside each other. Roll through to lock, if desired. This is the body of the bird.

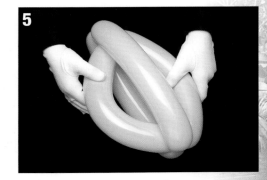

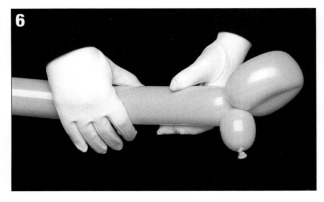

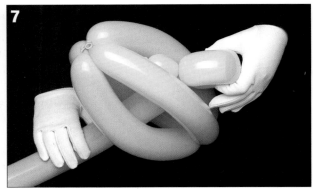

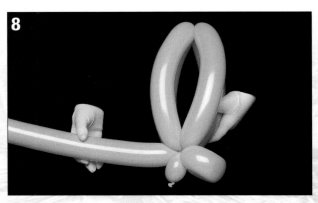

6) Using the second pink 260, make a 1/2-inch (1.25-cm) bubble (p.8) on the nozzle end, followed by a 2-inch (5-cm) loop twist (p.8) just beyond that.

7) Feed the bubbles of the second balloon through the middle of the football.

8) Twist at the back to make tail feathers.

9) Feed the tail through the inside of the football. Lock twist (p.9) to lock at the opposite end from the feathers.

10) Make a 1/2-inch (1.25-cm) bubble, and give it an ear twist (which won't hurt!).

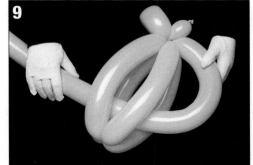

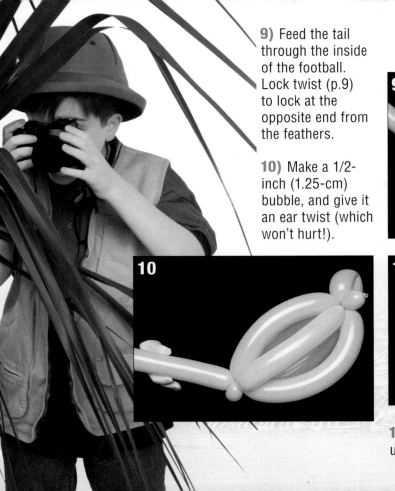

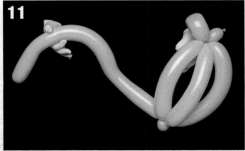

11) Curl (p.10) the long end for the neck until it looks like a question mark.

12) Now taking the black balloon, make a 1/2-inch (1.25-cm) bubble, then make a 2-inch (5-cm) loop twist right above that.
This is the first foot.
Squeeze air from the middle of the balloon to the tail to soften. Make another 1/2-inch (1.25-cm) bubble and 2-inch (5-cm) loop twist on the other end of the balloon for a second foot. Roll through to lock, if desired.

13) Find the center, and twist off for two legs.

14) Feed the legs through the bottom of the football, and twist around at the joint of the legs to attach.

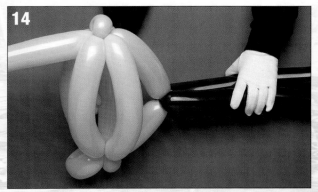

15) No good flamingo should be bowlegged, so let's fix that by cutting a 3-inch (7.5-cm) section of an uninflated black 260 and twisting it around one of the feet. Then twist the piece around the second foot to secure the legs.

16) Bend the legs, scrunching them together, to make knees.

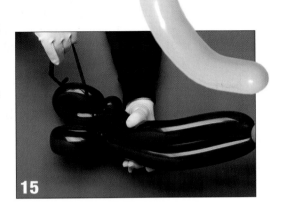

15

16

Can you say "pretty bird"?

SWAMPY CHOMPER

You don't have to wrestle this reptilian ruffian,
but you may want to keep your hand away from his mighty jaws!

1) Inflate two green 260s, leaving a 4-inch (7.5-cm) tail on one and a 2-inch (5-cm) tail on the second.

2) Make a 1-inch (2.5-cm) bubble (p.8) on the nozzle end of the first balloon, followed by two 2-inch (5-cm) bubbles.

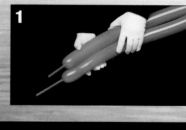

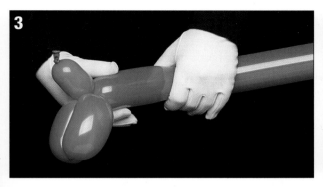

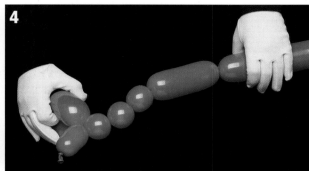

3) Lock twist (p.8) the 2-inch (5-cm) bubbles together for front legs.

4) Then make a string of three 3/4-inch (1.9-cm) bubbles and one 3-inch (7.5-cm) bubble.

5) Fold the string of bubbles over and lock.

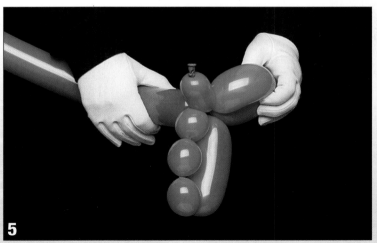

6

6) Make three 3/4-inch (1.9-cm) bubbles, and roll the string through the body to create two rows of scales.

7

7) Make two more 2-inch (5-cm) bubbles for the back legs, and twist together just as you did for the front legs.

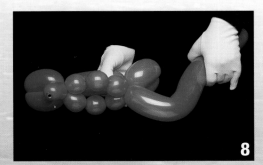

8

8) Scrunch up the middle of the remaining end.

9) Make a 1-inch (2.5-cm) bubble between the tail and the body, and ear twist (p.11) it to lock the bubbles in place.

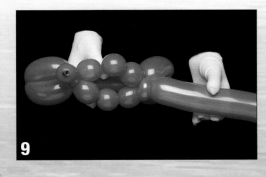

9

10) Using the second balloon, make another 1-inch (2.5-cm) bubble on the nozzle end.

11) Follow that with a 4-inch (10-cm) loop twist (p.8), locking it by twisting the 1-inch (2.5-cm) bubble through it.

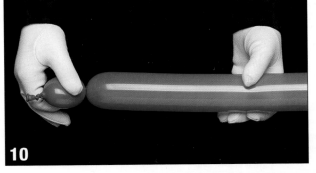

12) Make two 1 1/2-inch (3.8-cm) bubbles, and lock them into place for eyes.

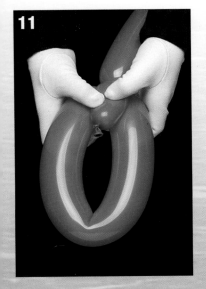

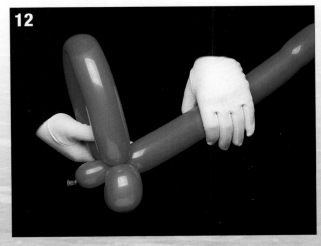

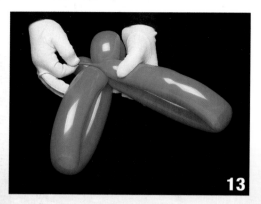

13) Squeeze the air to the tail, leaving a 1/2-inch (1.25-cm) tail, and make a loop, wrapping the tail end around the eyes.

14) Twist together the nozzle bubbles from each balloon.

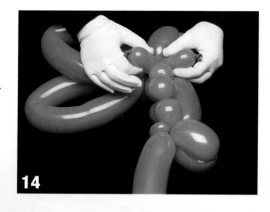

15) Position the balloons so the eyes are up, and so that the 1-inch (2.5-cm) bubbles are on the sides like jaws.

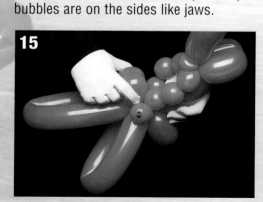

This one's more likely to snap than to pop!

JUNGLE JIM

How many monkeys does it take to get a giggle?
Just one, and you'll have a barrel full of laughs!

1) Inflate two 260s in the color of your choice, leaving a 3-inch (7.5-cm) tail on the first and a 4-inch (10-cm) tail on the second.

2) Make a 2-inch (5-cm) bubble (p. 8) and a 1/2-inch (1.25-cm) bubble on the nozzle end of the first balloon. Then ear twist (p.11) the 1/2-inch (1.25-cm) bubble.

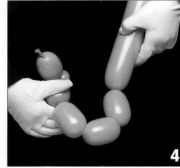

3) To make ears (and this is where you get the name "ear twist"), divide the ear twist into two bubbles.

4) Make a string of one 1-inch (2.5-cm) and three 1 1/2-inch (3.8-cm) bubbles.

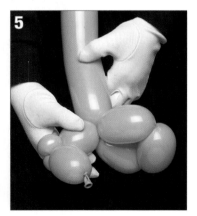

5) Twist the beginning and end of the strand together.

6) Push the face bubble through, locking the nozzle end around the neck. Tuck the nozzle inside the loop.

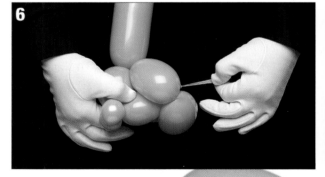

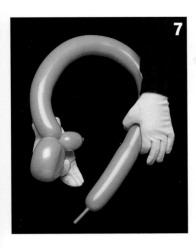

7) Using the second balloon, make a 1/2-inch (1.25-cm) bubble and a 2-inch (5-cm) loop twist (p.8) to form one hand, rolling it through to lock it. Then squeeze the balloon a little to soften (p.10) it.

8) Find the middle, estimating enough balloon with which to make another loop on the other end for the second hand. After making the hand, lock the tail end around the twist, cutting off any excess.

9) Make a twist (p.11) in the middle, and twist the arms around the other balloon at its last joint.

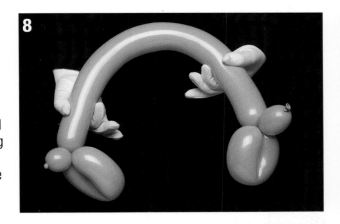

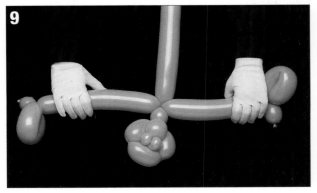

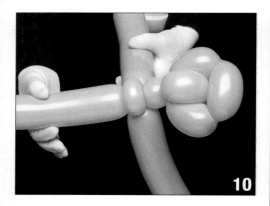

10

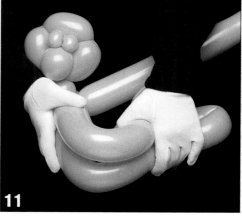

11

Your friends will go bananas, because this monkey has appeal!

10) Make an ear twist just below the joint.

11) Bend the arms to form the elbows on each side.

12) Form a 3-inch (7.5-cm) bubble below the arms for the body, and make a 3-inch (7.5-cm) loop twist for the feet. Then curl (p.10) the tail to give it shape.

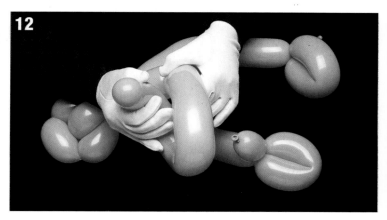

12

EIGHT THAT GREAT

If you're a sucker for sea creatures,
you'll think this one is nautical but nice!

1) Inflate four 260s, all the same color, leaving 1/2-inch (1.25-cm) tails on three and a 1-inch (2.5-cm) tail on the last one. Soften (p.10) all four balloons.

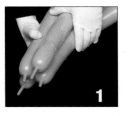

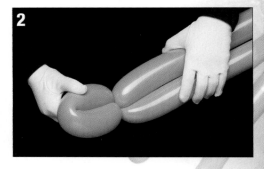

2) Measuring about 4 inches (10 cm) down on either side from the middle, pinch and twist each balloon that has a 1/2-inch (1.25-cm) tail.

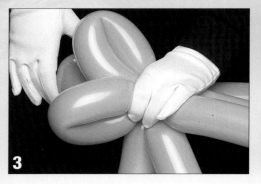

3

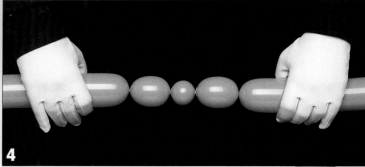

4

3) Then twist all three together at the joints. Your octopus (which is actually a hexapus at this point) has a head.

4) Using the fourth balloon, find the center. Then make a 1-inch (2.5-cm) bubble (p.8) just right of the center, followed by a 1/2-inch (1.25-cm) bubble and a 1-inch (2.5-cm) bubble.

5) Ear twist (p.11) the 1-inch (2.5-cm) bubbles together. These are the eyes that you will attach to the head.

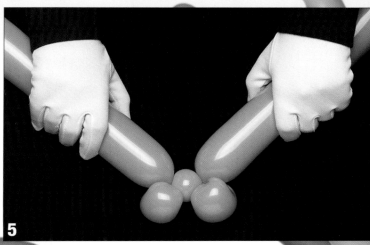

5

6) Slide the bubbles around the twist of the head

7) Twist the legs around the other six legs and position as needed.

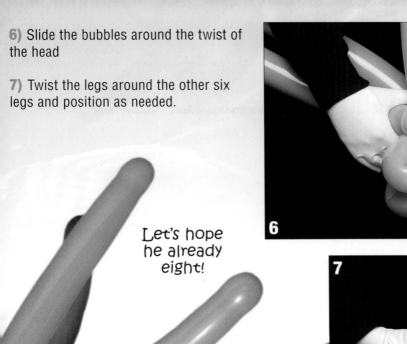

Let's hope he already eight!

6

7

HOPPY DAYS

Think you'd never kiss a frog?
This version may just win your heart!

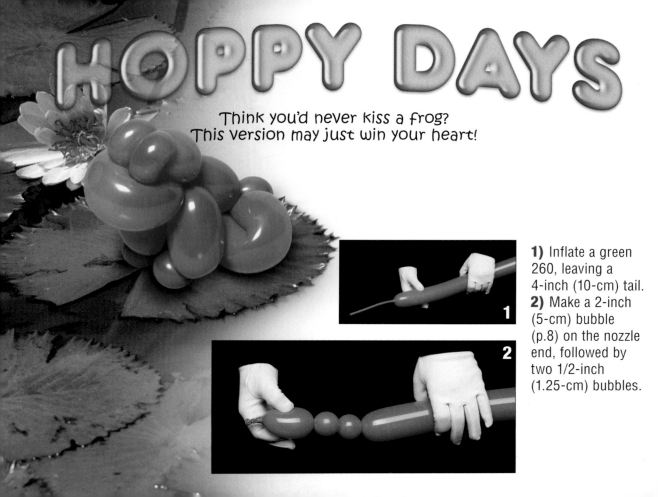

1) Inflate a green 260, leaving a 4-inch (10-cm) tail.
2) Make a 2-inch (5-cm) bubble (p.8) on the nozzle end, followed by two 1/2-inch (1.25-cm) bubbles.

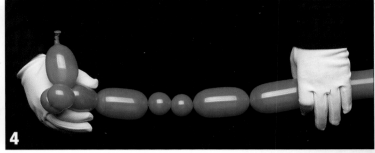

3) Twist the 1/2-inch (1.25-cm) bubbles together to make eyes. Ear twist them (p.11) to lock them in place.

4) Next make a 1-inch (2.5-cm) bubble, a 2-inch (5-cm) bubble, two 1/2-inch (1.25-cm) bubbles, and another 2-inch (5-cm) bubble.

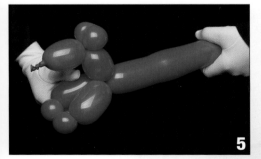

5) Twist the strand together at the joints of the 2-inch (5-cm) bubbles for the front legs and feet.

6) Fold down a 4-inch (10-cm) loop twist (p.8). Push the nozzle bubble through the loop.

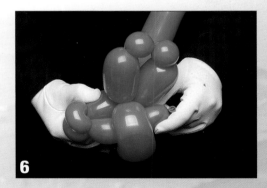

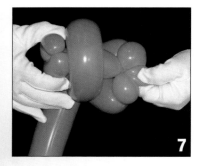

7) Make a 1/2-inch (1.25-cm) bubble on the nozzle end, then pull it down and lock it between the two 1/2-inch (1.25-cm) bubbles on the leg sections.

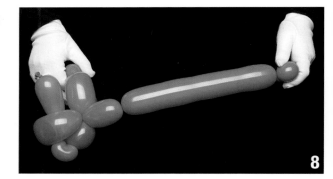

8) For the back, make a 1 1/2-inch (3.8-cm) bubble. Then squeeze the air to the end to soften the balloon (p.10), and make a 1/2-inch (1.25-cm) bubble on the very end.

9) Make a loop twist with the remaining section.

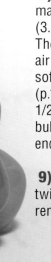

10) Find the center of the loop, and twist there (p.11).

11) Fold the loop into itself at the joints, and twist together at the joints to make back legs.

12) Stretch the nozzle around and between the legs, wrapping it around once to lock it in place.

Hoppy days are here again!

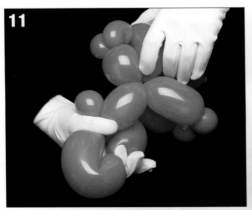

A HORSE, OF COURSE

This equine is so divine,
it's bound to be the mane event!

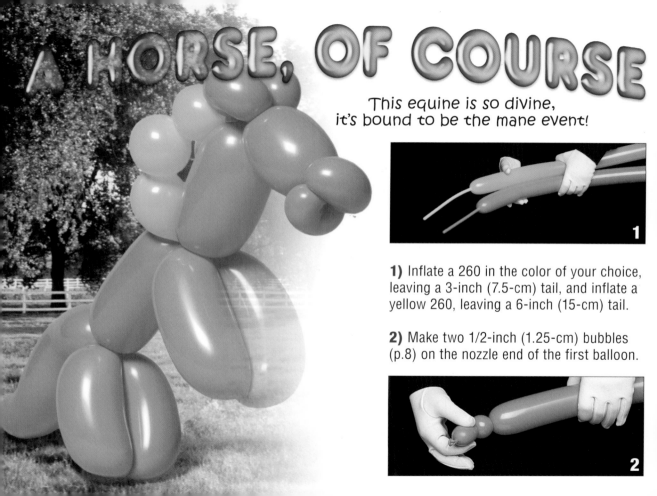

1) Inflate a 260 in the color of your choice, leaving a 3-inch (7.5-cm) tail, and inflate a yellow 260, leaving a 6-inch (15-cm) tail.

2) Make two 1/2-inch (1.25-cm) bubbles (p.8) on the nozzle end of the first balloon.

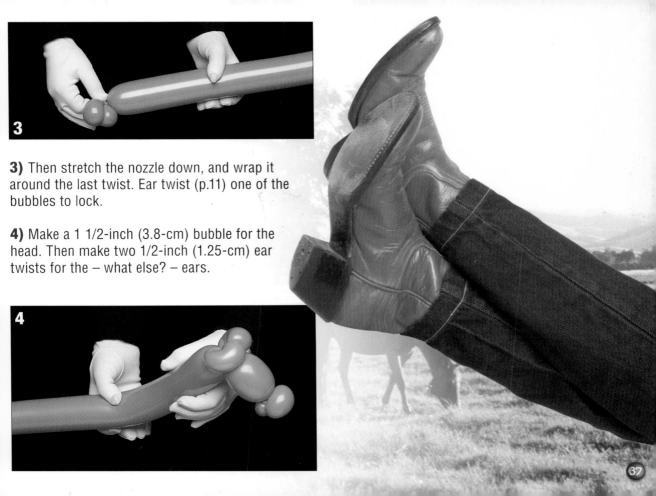

3) Then stretch the nozzle down, and wrap it around the last twist. Ear twist (p.11) one of the bubbles to lock.

4) Make a 1 1/2-inch (3.8-cm) bubble for the head. Then make two 1/2-inch (1.25-cm) ear twists for the – what else? – ears.

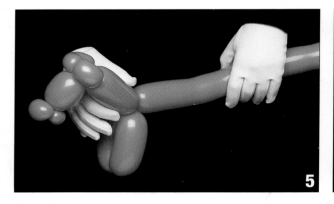

5

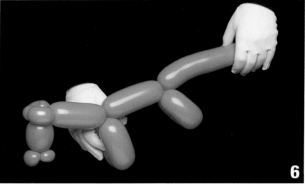

6

5) Make a 3-inch (7.5-cm) bubble for the neck. Now make two 3-inch (7.5-cm) bubbles for the legs, folding the second one down and twisting them together.

6) Make a 4-inch (10-cm) bubble for the body and two 3-inch (7.5-cm) bubbles for the back legs, locking them together as you did the front legs.

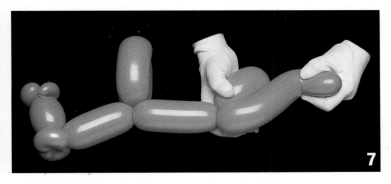

7) Fold the remaining tail section accordian-style into a Z, squishing it down to give it shape. You can also bend the body for a rounder back (so your horse doesn't look like a nag!).

8) Using the yellow balloon, make a string of six 1/2-inch (1.25-cm) bubbles, and tie the nozzle around the base to form a loop.

9) With the help of an adult, cut off the remaining section with scissors, tying the broken end to the nozzle.

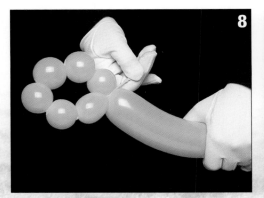

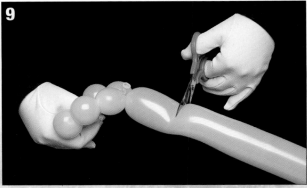

10) Slide the mane onto the horse from the underside of the neck at the top and bottom.

11) Pull it into position. Wrap the nozzle between the ears a couple of times to lock it.

Put on your chaps because this horse is ready to go!

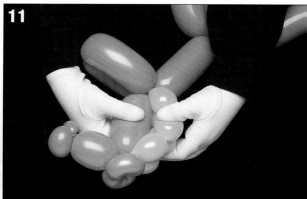

FOREVER FINS

This fish is so cute, it will have you hooked!

1) Inflate a 260 in the color of your choice, leaving a 1-inch (2.5-cm) tail.

2) Fold in half to find the center of the inflated portion. Make a 1-inch (2.5-cm) bubble (p.8) in that spot. Ear twist (p.11) the bubble.

3) Make another 1-inch (2.5-cm) bubble and ear twist right next to it to make fish lips. Then squeeze the air to the uninflated part of the balloon.

4) Make an X about 3 inches from either end, and twist together.

5) For a dorsal fin, squeeze a section in the middle of the top loop and release.

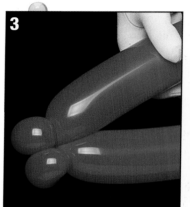

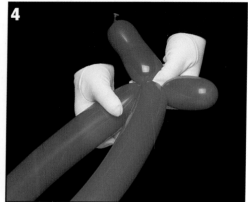

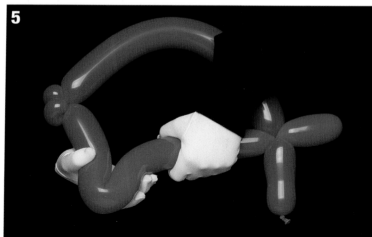

6

6) For eyes, inflate a 3-inch (7.5-cm) bubble in a 260 of a contrasting color, tying it off on either end, and cutting off the remainder with the help of an adult for another project.

7) Divide it in half, making two equal bubbles.

7

8) Insert the eyes about 2 inches (5 cm) above the mouth on the top loop of the balloon.

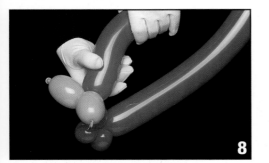

8

Now, don't be fishing for compliments!

HOT DOG!

This old dog doesn't need to learn any new tricks. He's a weiner every time!

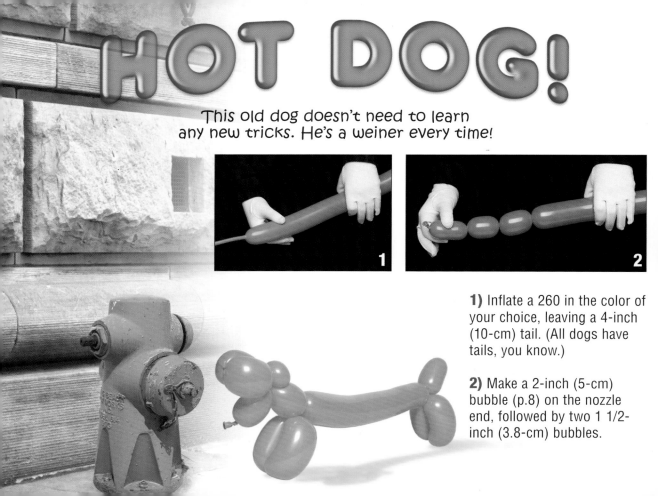

1) Inflate a 260 in the color of your choice, leaving a 4-inch (10-cm) tail. (All dogs have tails, you know.)

2) Make a 2-inch (5-cm) bubble (p.8) on the nozzle end, followed by two 1 1/2-inch (3.8-cm) bubbles.

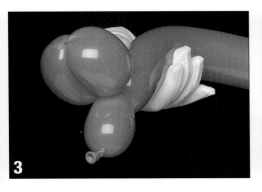
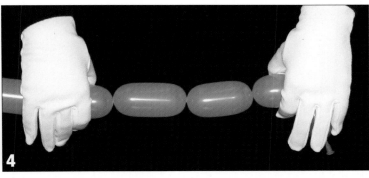

3) Fold the 1 1/2-inch (3.8-cm) bubbles down so their bases meet, and twist them together for ears.

4) Then make a 1-inch (2.5-cm) bubble and two 2-inch (5-cm) bubbles for the body and legs.

5) Fold the 2-inch (5-cm) bubbles down and twist together for front legs.

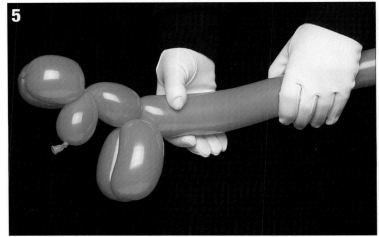

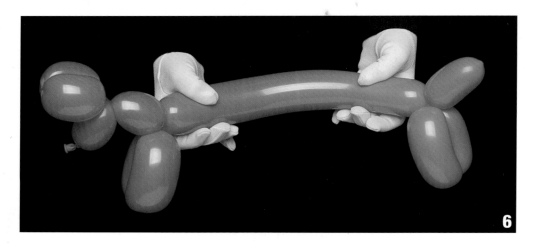

6) Measure 5 inches back from the tail end, and make two 2-inch (5-cm) bubbles and one 1-inch (2.5-cm) bubble (because 2+2+1 = 5, right?). Then fold the two 2-inch (5-cm) bubbles toward each other, and twist together at the base. You now have a four-legged friend.

This classic canine speaks for itself!

ICEBIRD

This dapper flapper
is king of cool!

1) Inflate a black 260, leaving a 2-inch (5-cm) tail.

2) Make a 1 1/2-inch (3.8-cm) bubble (p.8) and a 1-inch (2.5-cm) bubble on the nozzle end for a head. (All birds are bubble-heads, you know.) Ear twist (p.11) the 1-inch (2.5-cm) bubble.

3) For the body, start by making two 8-inch (20-cm) bubbles. Fold them down, and twist them together.

4) To complete the body, make another 8-inch (20-cm) bubble, and roll it through the first two to make a football shape.

5) Turn the head around so the rounder section is in the back, and your penguin is looking forward.

6) On the very tail of the remaining section, make a 1-inch (2.5-cm) bubble, and lock it around the base of the body.

7) Find the middle of that loop, and twist (p.11) there.

8) Push down at the middle with your thumb, and twist again to make two feet. Adjust position as needed.

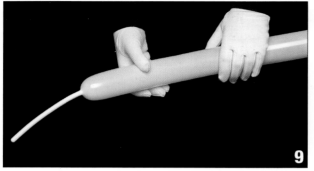
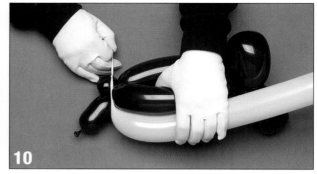

9) Your penguin still needs its distinctive white belly, so inflate a white 260 only about halfway.

10) Wrap the nozzle of the white balloon around the neck of the penguin twice, tucking it down to hide it.

11) Stretch the white balloon down the front of the body, and make a bubble that extends to the feet, twisting there and wrapping the joint around the feet.

12) With the help of an adult, cut off the unused section of balloon, and tie just below the bubble using scissors.

13) Twist the end of the white bubble around the feet to hide it.

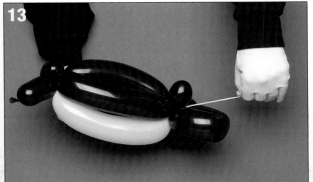

Waddle your friends think about that?

VENOMLESS VIPER

The only hiss you'll hear from this snake is if it springs a leak!

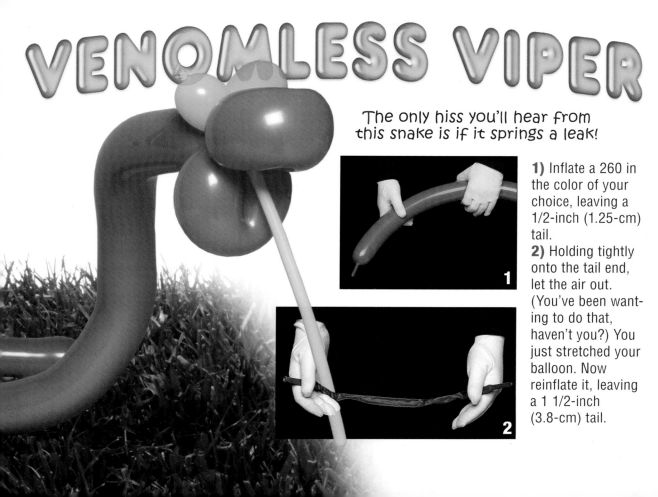

1) Inflate a 260 in the color of your choice, leaving a 1/2-inch (1.25-cm) tail.

2) Holding tightly onto the tail end, let the air out. (You've been wanting to do that, haven't you?) You just stretched your balloon. Now reinflate it, leaving a 1 1/2-inch (3.8-cm) tail.

3

4

3) Make a 2-inch (5-cm) loop twist (p.8) on the nozzle end, twisting the nozzle around and tying it onto the body. Your snake has half a mouth.

4) Make another 2-inch (5-cm) loop twist to complete the mouth.

5

Johnson & Johnson
FIRST AID KIT

5) Using a balloon of contrasting color, inflate a 2-inch (5-cm) bubble (p.8) at the nozzle end. Tie a knot on either side of the bubble. With the help of an adult, cut off the uninflated section of balloon with scissors. Set it aside.

53

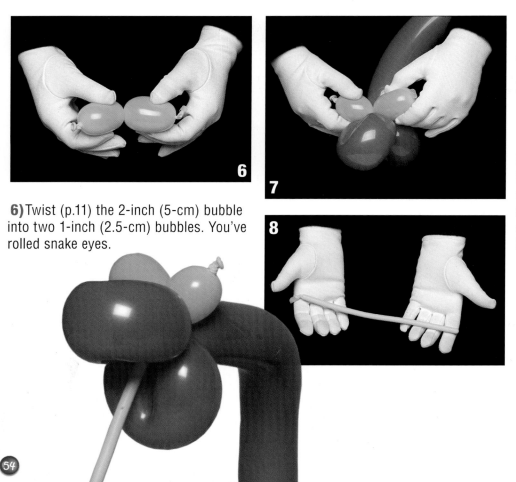

6
7

6) Twist (p.11) the 2-inch (5-cm) bubble into two 1-inch (2.5-cm) bubbles. You've rolled snake eyes.

8

7) Push the eyes through the twist of the mouth, and twist around to position.

8) Fill the remaining section of balloon, the one you set aside, with just a tiny bit of air. Tie a knot about an inch from the end.

54

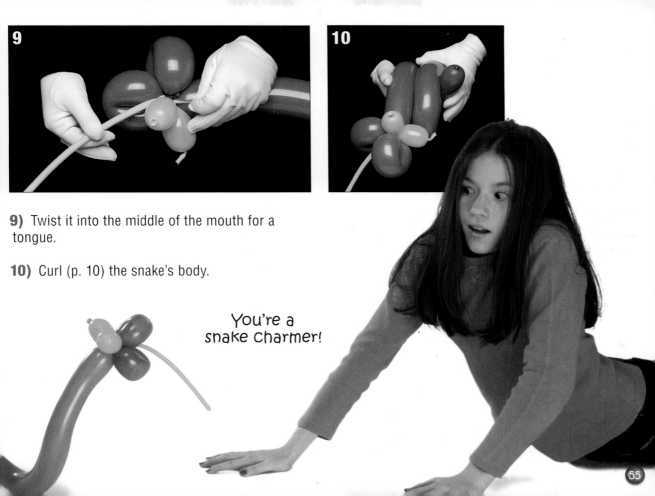

9) Twist it into the middle of the mouth for a tongue.

10) Curl (p. 10) the snake's body.

You're a snake charmer!

HARE-RAISER

With just a little sleight of hand,
you can make this rabbit magically appear!

1) Inflate a white 260 or a 260 in the color of your choice, leaving a 2-inch (5-cm) tail.

2) Make a 1 1/2-inch (3.8-cm) bubble (p.8) on the nozzle end for the face. Then make two 5-inch bubbles for floppy ears.

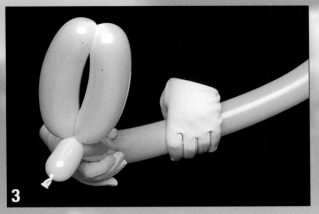

3) Fold the second one down, and twist them together.

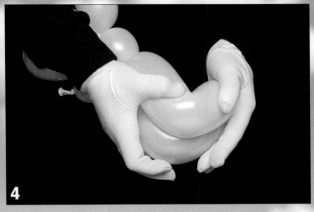

4) Curl (p.10) the ears.

57

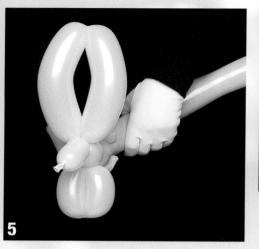

5

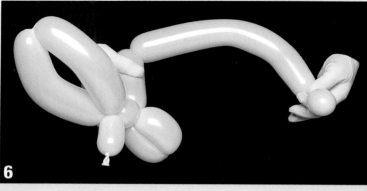

6

7

5) Make a 1-inch (2.5-cm) bubble for the neck, followed by two 2-inch (5-cm) bubbles for the front legs. Twist the 2-inch (5-cm) bubbles together as you did with the ears.

6) Make a 4-inch (10-cm) bubble for the body. On the very tip of the tail end, make a 1-inch (2.5-cm) bubble.

7) Fold the long section of balloon between the 4-inch (10-cm) and 1-inch (2.5-cm) bubbles in half, and twist the 1-inch (2.5-cm) bubble around the last twist of the 4-inch (10-cm) bubble.

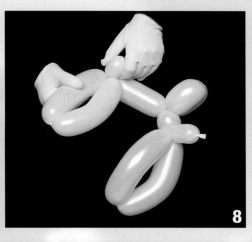

8) Twist the loop in half to form two back legs.

9) Tuck the front legs into the back legs.

That's no tricky rabbit!

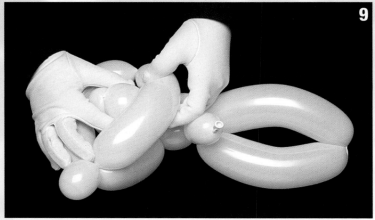

ONE YOU'LL NEVER FORGET

Don't pack up the peanuts for this pachyderm. Add air, and stir up a safari!

1) Inflate two gray 260s, leaving 2-inch (5-cm) tails.

2) Make a 1-inch (2.5-cm) bubble (p.8) on the nozzle end of one of the balloons, followed by an 8-inch (20-cm) loop twist (p.8) for the first ear. Twist the nozzle around the ear for a cleaner look. (How's he supposed to hear with messed up ears?)

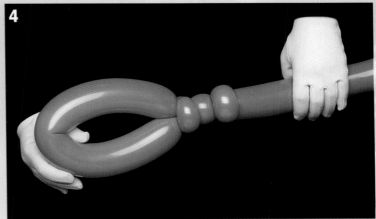

3) Make a 1/2-inch (1.25-cm) bubble, and ear twist (p.11) it.

4) Make two more 1/2-inch (1.25-cm) bubbles, ear twisting the second one.

5) Squeeze the air to the end of the balloon, and make a 1/2-inch (1.25-cm) bubble on the very end. (Tip: This is easier if you bend the tail toward you.) Then make a loop twist with the end section of balloon, locking the final 1/2-inch (1.25-cm) bubble around the last twist. This is the second ear.

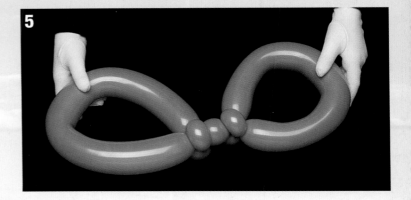

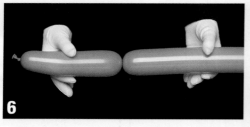

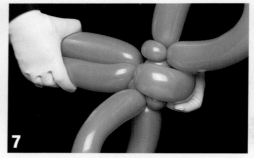

7) Wrap the section of balloon just above that between the ears, twisting around the joint of the trunk.

6) Using the second gray 260, make a 5-inch (12.5-cm) bubble on the nozzle end. That is the elephant's trunk.

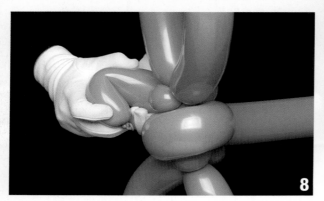

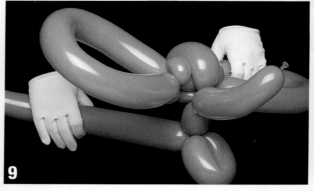

8) Curl (p.10) the trunk.

9) Make a 1-inch (2.5-cm) bubble for the neck, followed by a 2-inch (5-cm) loop twist for the front legs.

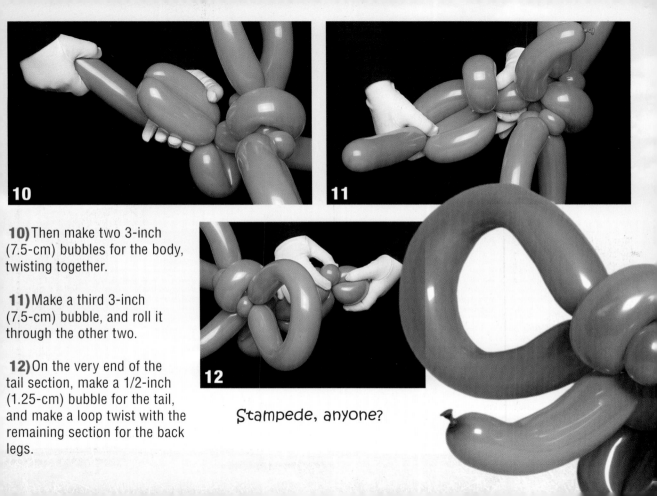

10) Then make two 3-inch (7.5-cm) bubbles for the body, twisting together.

11) Make a third 3-inch (7.5-cm) bubble, and roll it through the other two.

12) On the very end of the tail section, make a 1/2-inch (1.25-cm) bubble for the tail, and make a loop twist with the remaining section for the back legs.

Stampede, anyone?

Make Animals Appear Out of Thin Air!

Now that you have a few twists up your sleeve, you're ready to become everyone's favorite party animal! But why stop at our ideas, and why not come up with a few of your own? Let your menagerie evolve into a world of dogfish and allipuses. Or create your own new class of critters! Your air pets are at your command. So, make like a giant lizard, and let your imagination saur!